IN THE GARDEN OF THE
THREE ISLANDS

IN THE GARDEN OF THE THREE ISLANDS

Maria Luisa B. Aguilar-Cariño

ASPHODEL PRESS
MOYER BELL

WAKEFIELD, RHODE ISLAND AND LONDON

Published by Asphodel Press
Copyright © 1995 by Maria Luisa B. Aguilar-Cariño

All rights reserved. No part of this publication may be reproduced or transmitted in any form or by any means electronic or mechanical, including photocopying, recording or any information retrieval system, without permission in writing from Asphodel Press, Kymbolde Way, Wakefield, Rhode Island 02879 or 112 Sydney Road, Muswell Hill, London N10 2RN.

First Edition

**LIBRARY OF CONGRESS
CATALOGING-IN-PUBLICATION DATA**

Cariño, Maria Luisa B. Aguilar-, 1961–
In the Garden of the Three Islands :
poems / Maria Luisa B. Aguilar-Cariño. — 1st ed.
    p. cm.
ISBN 0-55921-117-2 (pb)
1. City and town life—Philippines—Baguio—Poetry.
2. Baguio (Philippines)—Poetry.　I. Title.
PS3553.A686I5　1994
811'.54—dc20
94-13803　CIP

Printed in the United States of America. Distributed in North America by Publishers Group West, P.O. Box 8843, Emeryville, CA 94662, 800-788-3123 (in California 510-658-3453) and in Europe by Gazelle Book Services Ltd., Falcon House, Queen Square, Lancaster LA1 1RN England 524-68765.

CONTENTS

Preface | 1

IN THE GARDEN OF THE THREE ISLANDS
Sansho-en: In the Garden of the Three Islands | 5
Vendor of Sweets | 7
Gabi | 9
Dinakdakan | 12
Letter for All Souls' Day | 14
White Flag | 16
Crimes of Opportunity | 17
Winter Forecast | 19
Passage | 23
At the Adler Planetarium | 27
Farewell | 28

CARTOGRAPHY
Old World | 33
At Hann's Cliff | 36
From the Diary of D. Burnham | 38
Arcanum | 40
The Secret Language | 42
Piano Teacher | 44
Death Anniversary | 46
Dissections | 48
Insomnia | 50
Leave-Taking | 52
Curse | 53
Encounter | 55
In Guisad Valley | 57
Legend | 59
Cartographer | 61

CONFIGURING THE GODS AND OTHER POEMS
A Sense of Balance | 65
Remembering a Death | 67
September | 69
Configuring the Gods | 71
The Alchemist's Stone | 72
Vigil | 73
Roses from the Sea | 75
Adagio | 76
Clarity | 77
A Weaving Song | 78
Woman from the North | 80

DISCLOSURES
Mount Santo Tomas | 85
Improvisation | 86
Monsoon | 87
From Eve | 89
Mateo | 90
Poem for Grandmothers, Mothers and Daughters | 91
Harvest-Eve | 92
Picture-Taking in Besao | 93
From an Album | 94
Omaira | 96
Burying Kinja | 98
Thirty-Third Year | 100
At Maryheights | 101
After Movies | 103
Coming of Age | 104

SIGHTINGS

Sightings | 109
Parchment | 111
Openwork | 112
The Send-Off | 113
Sagada | 115
Child Asleep | 116
Lake Danom | 117
Untitled | 118
On the Boulevard | 119
Wish | 120
Passages | 121
Last Supper | 122
Tryst | 124
Dancer at the Barre | 126
Landscapes | 127

PREFACE

In January 1990 while living in Baguio City in the Philippines, I applied for a Fulbright fellowship abroad, rekindling desires which, like everything in my life up to that point, had been carefully regularized and prioritized. I had been teaching for ten years and had given birth to three daughters in the same interim. Throughout this time I continued to write my poetry, joined literary competitions and published occasionally. My "secret world" of words fed me, but I found it difficult to clear spaces in the day during which I could bring it to completion. What is most memorable about those years is the physicality of my experience of writing, how it was so bound up with actual bodily sensations that brought the materiality of writing practice into acute relief. Once I awoke at three in the morning to breast-feed my second daughter; while she finished suckling, I sat in a chair and waited—and then realized that now I actually had time to write out the shape of a poem that had been forming in my mind. As cocks crowed in the dark, I moved to the desk and wrote, my daughter still cradled to my left breast.

Years later, in 1990, I contemplated with my husband the prospect of a fellowship abroad. Our daughters were 10, 8, and 3 years old; were they strong enough to let me go? Was I?

In July, just a few months after we had moved into our new home, two earthquakes registering 8.8 on the Richter scale struck in quick succession. In three minutes, our retaining wall cracked from ceiling to floor, causing part of the roof and the second floor to cave in with it.

In answer to a desperate prayer, our family was unscathed. But everything familiar in the landscape was levelled, and with it, the hopes we'd built would have to be erected anew. And then I received the Fulbright grant for '92, a five-year doctoral program in creative writing at the University of Illinois in Chicago. "Go," my husband told me, despite the remonstrations from well-meaning individuals, "otherwise one day you'll wake up, look in the mirror, and not like what you see."

And so I went, or rather came—and the poems in the section "In the Garden of the Three Islands," written in my first year of "exile" in America, are but an extension of the original impetus which worked on me years ago—to study the landscapes which the self inhabits and traverses, and which in turn work on memory and consciousness in such instructive ways. In my current journeys in America, I am a writer who is trying to carve a space of my own in a landscape that often insists on the surrender of symbols of allegiance at some tollgate or other: I should be either completely foreign/Asian/Filipino, or Asian *American/*Filipino *American*. But what if I refuse? What if, like Salman Rushdie, I would rather say, "I buck, I snort, I whinny, I rear, I kick. Ropes, I do not choose between you. . . . I choose neither of you, and both. Do you hear? I refuse to choose."

Doubtless more crossroads shall present themselves, and I will need to propel myself in some direction. For now, reflecting on the title of this volume I think of the first two islands on which mortals can leave the imprint of their physical bodies—the turning of leaves in passing, the unlatching of gates. And I think of the third island, the one which only spirits inhabit, the one which has no footbridge but shimmers in the distance the same way words call to the soul from across the abyss.

I thank the poets Ralph Mills, Jr. and Michael Anania for bringing my work to the attention of Moyer Bell. And I thank Jennifer Moyer for the encouragement to continue walking my voice out into the challenging world.

Maria Luisa B. Aguilar-Cariño
1 January 1995
Chicago

IN THE GARDEN
OF THE THREE ISLANDS

SANSHO-EN:
IN THE GARDEN OF THE THREE ISLANDS

The leaves of the gingko open,
tiny fans
fracturing light into
a likeness of repose.

In the stone garden
toothed circles signify
pools deep enough
to drown in, the white
weight of clouds,
a silence
obliterating sight.

Everything condenses:
the first
island envelops
its shuttered house
in leafage, the well
shapes its mouth
in a continual gesture
to unslaked
thirst.

Past the willow
hung bridge, past
the oleanders and darkening
moss, the formal sprigs recede

toward the second island,
the third, where spirits
disrobe in moonlight—
love having acquired
the transparency of grief
or loss.

It is at this
moment I will
myself to you,
the air sharp
with crickets' cries,
a clairvoyance
of no consolation.

VENDOR OF SWEETS

You seek her out in the noonday sun,
all your pores flowering sweat.
Under the arches at the corner
of Mabini and Harrison she squats,
sucking a brown wad of tobacco.
The corners of her mouth glisten
with saliva, pleasuring the wind-borne
smell of fish and scallions
from an open-air café.

Above the tattered mat
bearing a syllabary of wild roots
and charms—snakebone, powders
of venomous color, dried
flowers the size of balled-up
fetuses—her eyes float deep
in their leathered pouches:
one bright, one moonless.

Just once, briefly, you pass
your hand across your navel.
She understands the heat
that billows unbidden to your cheeks,
the clasp of metal new
around your finger.

Very swiftly (so you must pay attention),
she thumbs a twist of dry leaves, a stump
whorled almost in recognizable
configurations of passion.

Each night you scrape a little
of the fibrous bark into your lover's tea.
Each night you steep the leaves
and loosening limbs in tepid water,
inhaling and releasing scent
into the warm room.

Tendrils of hair quicken, the heart
begins its discomposing rhythms.
Beneath night's unlidded eye
the crush of berries on moist flesh
trickles from neck to breast,
through parted thighs.

GABI

1

Three sunrises
distant, at the river's
lip, the women unwrap
their heads
from many-times-
starched bandannas.

In the shimmering
heat, pleats
of hair unloose
a fortnight's rain
of dust, lice-eggs—

and the fair one
steps, body
beaconing wind,
into the stunned
shallows.

Take heed, say the women.
Never bathe
by moonlight. Fasten
your shutters, burn
votive candles—
around your neck,
string scapulars.

Trailing a spasm
of fish, moth wings
and beggar's ticks,
the river god breaks
through the wet
underworld of dreams.

Now her feet swell,
they grow
heavy and waterlogged,
the green sap rising
to her eyes.

2

Tonight we'll sup
on fairy tales:
a dish of boiled
gabi, whose leaves resemble
blue-green hearts
fed on rain, on waters
of darkest jealousy;
plumes of the red *labuyo*,
ginger roots that once
were nuggets of gold.

Departing
from the story,
I invent
no refusals. Look
how lovingly I watch
you shape each
spoonful to your mouth,
each piece steamed
to translucence. Later,
the paroxysms of warmth,
the foreknowledges
of taste.

> gabi — a plant with broad, heart-shaped leaves and
> a thick, waxy stem; it grows in shallow water and is
> used in many Philippine vegetable dishes, one popular one
> being heavily laced with coconut milk and
> siling labuyo (small, hot, red peppers); labuyo
> is also the name given to the wild rooster

DINAKDAKAN

(for Mama Tet)

This could be
the supermarket of your dreams,
the shelves slick and
showy with fruit, wide-
mouthed mason jars of herring,
rice grains longer
than your fingernail.

Our shopping cart would quickly swell
with breads whose names till now
were fable: rye, stone-ground
wheat, poppyseed buns;
the brie and camembert
longed for at Christmastime
instead of the yearly *queso
de bola*; the Spam and corned
beef worth a whole week's pay.

And then I think of you
as on a trip to market long ago:
the marvel was not merely
how the wind lifted our hair,
knifed raw the flesh of our mouths,
wrists, cheeks—how our rubber
boots were worthless in steady rain
and slippery mud.

It was you, plunging a bare
arm into a pail of still-breathing milkfish,
certain which had the sweetest belly;
knowing where to find
tamarind pods cracking
out of their rinds for ripeness,
the lemon grass for boiling
with white rice, the river snails
to steep into a heady broth.
(We extricated these with safety
pins, smacking lips, fingers.)

Among the rows of plastic-sealed
aseptically packaged food,
I stare and stare, imagining flat,
dried, salted fish-shapes pressed
between the cereal boxes,
fresh blood and entrails forming
a dark pool on the white linoleum.

Above the click and hum
of computerized cash registers
I hear your singing knife
slice pigs' ears paper-thin,
your fork twirl thick
clouds of boiled brain and minced
shallots for the evening meal.

LETTER FOR ALL SOULS' DAY

A smell like rain
descends upon the flowerbeds
to make the grass
distinct, more pointed.
I wake from a dream
of earth pelting my face,
the memory of you
released, with a tug.

Here, by the lake
throwing off blue
scales of water,
the leaves detach themselves
from out-thrust branches
slowly, the difficult
sap still heavy
in their veins.

Your eyes were the last
kindness, unfaltering
even as your face stiffened
into a shape beyond
finality, your body
yielding its old wounds,
giving up all
indentations of flesh
to view.

I want to imagine
you floating away
on unshadowable water,
away from the bowls of food
and garlands of flowers, away
from the rising sea of smoke
and candlewax—

your heart now
lighter than its papery
vessel, its last
bloody filament
on the white pillow
the only thread to tell me
where you have gone.

WHITE FLAG
(National Gallery of Art, after Elsworth Kelly)

> *I am not where I think,*
> *I think where I am not*
> —Jacques Lacan

Under the waxy mounds
suggesting snowdrifts or clouds,
the outlines of stars lie sealed.
The panelled seams hold forth
a lipless and tentative geography
whose borders and valleys
our tongues would scroll.
Breath by indrawn breath, the steam
of syllables spoken in another
country slides down our throats:
in Vienna, lightning rips
through the sky, exploding
on the *mardi gras* parade
of Modibo's gown. Pots and pans
rattle, the grandfather turns
in bed. In his dream
lilies turn into fireflies
fading at daylight's touch.
In Korea, a child pushes eel-like
through rippling water, searching
for its mother. The river
beds are bright, speckled
with sand and the snails
that have crawled their patient
way from Africa and beyond to here,
to these white shores.

CRIMES OF OPPORTUNITY

My neighbor leaves
for his shift, badge
glinting on his blue
regulation uniform. Last
Monday he read me his blotter
report: a chink in morning's
first hour, pale white
underwear and sunlight
plaited around the girl's face.
If you don't look
sometimes there is hope
the rapist will let you go
with minimal damage.

Walking to work I see
the usual spray of broken
glass printing the sidewalk,
cerveza negra or Southern
Comfort. This is its own
strident bulletin,
challenging the assured
click of heels
on the pavement. Caught
in the corner of the eye,
a slight movement in
the undisturbed houses,
the barely discernible
rearrangement of flowered
curtains.

And what if a tree falls,
unwitnessed,
in the forest?
Are the body's wounds
generous enough
to contain the narrative
traces of its collapse,
the outlines of warm liquid
trickling over the stones
waiting to be read?

In the evenings I open
my third-floor windows,
releasing the day's collected
blankness from the walls.
Leaning out, I wish
for something unlikely—
to trust in a brief
scattering of music, a hymn
hoisting itself above
the burdened clothes-
lines and the corner store
where the odors of roast
meat mingle with sweat
and drunken laughter.

I turn the lock, wedge
a chair against the door.

WINTER FORECAST

At the Omnimax
seventy speakers recreate
earth's rumblings
in full stereo.
The camera skims past
the tops of shuddering palms
on the concave screen.
Mesmerized, the audience follows
the bulge straining
to release,
through viscera of rock,
a curdled lava-flood.

On temple lawns
in faraway Borobodur
loincloth-clad dancers
lock arms and legs
within a ring.
Lurching bodies enact
a battle of demons
to frenzied chants
and peal of cymbals.

Further east,
Pinatubo heaves.
Swollen
rivers overflow
monsoon-choked banks.

First, the bridges go; then
the chicken coops
with their frantic
occupants, the tin
roofs and clapboard
houses, the carabaos
doomed
in their eternal
slowness.

Towns tumble
into the thick stew, 1.4 billion
cubic meters of rampaging
mud and ash unchecked
by sandbags and lunar
tides, sundering all
known and future
geographies.

Lungs full
to bursting, villagers
flee, shepherding children
and bleating goats
through air thicker
and more pointillist
than in Seurat's *Sunday
at La Grande Jatte.*

The sky splits,
raining ash heavier
than sins atoned for
at Lent: some
of the landlord's grain
taken in stealth
for gruel, water
for the cracked fields
and parched lips;
waifs thrusting just-
budding breasts out
at the highway's edge.

A hemisphere
away, the *Old Farmer's
Almanac* conjures
the year's glacial
turning. Survival
is possible
with thinsulate and fleece-
lined boots. Beyond
the double storm
windows, the prophesied cold
descends—a snowfall
of inverted ciphers
over the dark
lake. Somewhere
on the wintering landscape,

white-tailed deer step
through bracken and mullein
leaf, through imponderable
drifts.

PASSAGE

*(to the memory of
Amadeo Belmonte, pediatrician)*

> *Here is your path to God, who
> has no name, whose hand is
> invisible . . .*
> —Rilke

1

Snow falls, thick
as unparsed speech,
assembling landscape,
a night for imagining
a newborn's faraway
and desolate cry
quavering up the ridged
backs of hills.

In the bone-white
nursery, the infants come
swimming through the portals
to your fingers' summons. Damp
with the effluvium of salt
they let you slough
their streaked and creamy
wrappings off, administer
light, a swoon of air.

2

Soon, despite themselves
they are hungry for the world.
They make fists, curl their toes,
make sucking noises—
thirstier than the trees
whose leaves have spiralled away
to emptiness, whose veins
and taproots have been
leached for winter's rites.

In the days and nights
that follow, we bring
our children to you, sometimes
pink and obedient as heart-
beats, sometimes weightless
and struggling for breath.
We rock and weep
in a forest of uncertainty,
expand in the knowledge
of each moment
after birth.

We weave blood-
and-moth-wing dreams,
sip the broth of clams.
Nights we spend tending

cocoons, collecting breast
milk, watching light
pool beneath
the edges of the fontanelle.

3

Beloved-of-God,
the grandmothers
and aunts strike
their breasts, blame
each other for not
keeping closer watch
at your wedding.

Did a freak wind
extinguish a taper
as you bent to kiss
your smiling bride?
Much later, did a winedrop
slip, crimson with portent
and unnoticed, down the hand-
sewn panels of lace
on her gown?

4

On cold mornings
the children make
angels, leaping
without hesitation
into the snow.
Faces turned
to the sky, they land
on their backs. Arms flail
up and down describing
wings, colored butterflies
pinned to a lamina.

Home, as here,
each breath flowering
from their mouths
returns the body to this
recollection of birth—
the soul issuing forth
from the throat and rising,
rising above
the battered
trees.

AT THE ADLER PLANETARIUM

Only in darkness
do we begin to see:
the sky shading
to cyclamen, truest
of night-colors,
Polaris a bright
droplet hung—
this dome a cup
emptying desire
down our upraised
throats. Poisoned
beyond loss, we stride
into the wind,
renouncing the crowned
buildings, their tenuous
disguises of light.

FAREWELL

All morning long I have savored
the thought of this repast
arriving on boats of light
balsa wood—the fragile
strips of color,
the fragrant names
bundled in rice and sun-
dried seaweed,
mustard a sharp rosette
melting on my tongue.

A universe implodes
on the plate as smoke
trails over our heads
and the rattle of tin resounds
in a faraway kitchen.

We drain our cups,
rest our fingertips
on the brown straw mats
as if on skin,
knowing this moment
like the lake just beyond
the scrim of vision
resists translation.

How easy to forget,
to slide into your arms
without resistance
the way fish trust
their bodies to
undercurrents.

But we don't speak
of how we won't see each
other again, of how
the wind in my ears rises
from my country,
humid and insistent.

Here come the warm
towels offering erasure,
a way to blot the last
traces of salt and oil
so, undamaged,
we can float
free of each other.

Like the girl in the folk-
tale I wonder
what it will feel like
to be turned away from Heaven
for holding back one
grain of rice
under my tongue.

CARTOGRAPHY

OLD WORLD

From old photographs, it is easy
To imagine the world without peaks,
Even and benign, innocent
Of mercenary purpose.
In the yellowing prints
Any hint of mountains
Is lost in distant shadow,
Or perhaps the sky was simply
Wider than it is now.

Like tourists revisiting
The scenes of an old
Amnesia, we venture
Within the frames:

At the center, the main street,
Raked clean, looks strangely expectant;
A footpath, barely visible,
Leads to the watering-hole.
The salt licks for the deer
Wait in their customary places,
Whole flocks of sparrows
Flick their wings over the water
And disappear.

In the Chinaman's store,
Under damp towels,
Balls of yeast rise

Like pale moons
Beside trays of liquor
And tinned fish.

In Lucban, where now
No oranges can flower
Except in the wish of the mother
Tending her sick child
Behind the scarred walls of
A tenement shanty,
The stars continue their ancient
Surveillance.

All this seems
Light years away.

We move to the window
To watch day break, amazed
At the discovery
Of our assailability.

On the rooftop, floors above us,
Early morning golfers meander
Through fictive greenery,
Swinging their arms
As though to dissipate
The most exquisite
Of boredoms.

In this aerie we nurse our wings,
Too exhausted to discern
What haste propels the brown
Cameo figures pushing, at precarious tilt,
Cartfuls of vegetables and flowers
Through the asphyxiated streets.
Their voices rise and fall,
Seeking the interstices
Of time.

AT HANN'S CLIFF

23 February 1904;
Camp One, Kennon Road

"Several parties of native laborers
on reaching the top of the cliff looked
over the edge and turned, refusing
to go farther."
—from Baguio Memoirs

My foreman praises
The sureness of my footing,
The patience with which
I crumble the rocky soil
With my pick.
Even the ends of his moustache
Bristle with energy
When he shakes my hand,
Calls me his best man
And promises a raise in pay.
I almost believe him
Until I remember
The week he called me
A damned monkey
For coming down with malaria.
Somehow I am alive.
It is not that I
Have great courage.
These footbridges that
Like odd centipedes
Circle the edge
Of Hann's Cliff
Sway in the wind.

What I do with my hands
Is distraction: I look
At the patched textures of stones
And the color of weeds.
The metal and heft of my implements
Are things I can understand.

When the noon bell rings
I rest as lightly as I can.
I eat my ration of meat
And rice, and stare
Past the purple mountains
At the almost unvarying sky.
I try not to listen too closely
To the river boiling more
Than a hundred feet beneath.

It is in my dreams
That my spirit flies
Over these ravines,
Looking for my bones.
As we snake our way up, I call
On the names of my ancestors
And constantly seek a sign
Of blessing amid the trees,
In the call of birds.

FROM THE DIARY OF D. BURNHAM
DECEMBER 1904

>   *quorum deus venter est*
>   —Fray Lorenzo Fondevila, 1834

Atop the crenellated trail
I survey this stupendous gift
Such as no man has received.

Already the nightmare
Of days poisoned with heat,
Mosquitoes, and tainted water
Dissolves in the astringent air,
Whole skyfuls of it aswirl
With the effulgence of dusk.

Tonight I shall seek the core
Of this wilderness and
With my pen, subdue it. I have
Such plans! It will be
As though the very trees
Will have learnt civility
And grace, leaning genteelly
Upon the wind, in rows
Among the stately buildings,
Along the parkways
And the roads.

This will be a city
To astound the mind:
Magisterial, orderly,
Thoughtful of amenities

That civilized men
In a hostile land
Take comfort in.

But to impose cold, level
Regularity—such would be
Unworthy of this challenge.

No, I shall leave unretouched
The brutish designs of rocks
And ridges. On these shall flower
(Years from now, a charming prospect)
Cottages and country houses,
Trellises triumphant
With roses and clematis.

From their open windows
I can almost hear the delicate
Strains of a waltz, or a slow
And dreamy foxtrot
Silencing the chatter
Of monkeys in the trees

While, hinge by hinge, the leaf-screens
Round the garden open
And dark-haired, dark-eyed
Children wrapped in bark
Approach the light, lips
In wonder parted.

ARCANUM

> *the cat unsheathes its claws*
> *the world turns*
> —Sylvia Plath

The rains have come upon us
As they have all these years,
But in the wrong season.

We had not noticed
How the horizon
Was calculating this
Betrayal, in its receding wake
Taking the trees,
The pliant earth, the streams
Of all our childhoods.

In the beginning,
The river spoke
Its secret heartbeat
Only to us. The wind's
Every mottled tremor
Passed through each pore.

Down our calendar
We moved, marking
With sheaves of grain,
Birdcalls, the scaled
Progress of the lizard
From stone to stone,
The dark coursing of

Knowledge in our blood.
This language we understood
And relinquished.

Now we forage for weeds
And the smallest of stones,
Throats parched,
Dreamless.

THE SECRET LANGUAGE

I have learned your speech,
Fair stranger; for you
I have oiled my hair
And coiled it tight
Into a braid as thick
And beautiful as the serpent
In your story of Eden.

For you, I have covered
My breasts and hidden,
Among the folds of my surrendered
Inheritance, the beads
I have worn since girlhood.

It is fifty years now
Since the day my father
Took me to the school in Bua,
A headman's terrified
Peace-gift. In the doorway,
The teacher stood, her hair
The bleached color of corn,
Watching with bird-eyes.

Now, I am Christina.
I am told I can make lace
Fine enough to lay upon the altar
Of a cathedral in Europe.
But this is a place
That I will never see.

I cook for tourists at an inn;
They praise my lemon pie
And my English, which they say
Is faultless. I smile
And look past the window,
Imagining father's and grandfather's cattle
Grazing by the smoke trees.
But it is evening, and these
Are ghosts.

In the night,
When I am alone at last,
I lie uncorseted
Upon the iron bed,
Composing my lost beads
Over my chest, dreaming back
Each flecked and opalescent
Color, crooning the names,
Along with mine:
Binaay, Binaay.

PIANO TEACHER
For Concepcion Atienza

Who can tell how many fingers
Swept into position
Under your gaze, or trembled
Through a *solfeggio?*

Those afternoons rest
In memory, so much like blooms
Of an indecipherable hue
Under a dome of glass:

And there you sit, one hand
On the far end of the keyboard
To catch all my slipped notes.
Afterwards there is weak tea
With little white cubes of sugar.
In the moist air of your kitchen
My mother helps you with English.

Later, you speak of your lost
Girlhood. You show photographs
Where you laugh in your new straw hat
With cousins in Antipolo; in another,
You wave your hanky from the boat
That will take you and your parents
For a holiday in Barcelona.

From the shadows, among the hatboxes
Smelling faintly of *agua de colonia*,
Almost forgotten amid the talk,
Suddenly I understand how
To play the *kundiman*.

I close my eyes, imagining you
In a long, heavy frock
In the walled garden of the *colegio*
Where you learned music
And how it cannot entirely
Diminish love.

DEATH ANNIVERSARY

In this, the twentieth year,
The lines of your face
Have blurred in my mind.
What remains is something
Indefinable
Yet always present,
A soft grey film spreading
Across the outer wall,
Presaging rain,
The songs of cicadas,
And various mossy growths.

I would know you
If I met you in my dreams.
In these visions,
It is always night.
All the crimson in your hair
Has fallen away,
And the necromancy
Of my words
Returns your limbs,
Whole and perfumed
With the scent of lilies.

What they say happened
Has assumed the substance
Of legend.
Strangers pore over
The strands of your murder
as though it were someone's
Invention.

Through the syllables
I listen for your
Footfall.
I am nine again,
Reeling
At the portent
Of blood spilt
Upon the floor.

DISSECTIONS

> *Dr. Jose M. Cariño (a native Ibaloi) . . . went abroad in February 1914 to continue his medical studies . . . he was awarded an MD degree and for one year served as resident physician in the Pittsburgh General Hospital.*
> —Baguio Memoirs

The instruments on the tray
Lie disinfected, washed too
In this grey light
That substitutes for morning.
On the table before me,
A body, terrible gift,
Awaits undoing by the scalpel:

First, I touch you
With my eyes, inhaling
An already imagined forgiveness
For my inexpert fumbling.

But no shadow of pain or outrage
Darkens your face
As I invade the ribcage,
Freeing no wind
In the leafless branches of lung.

The heart folds keep forever
The dark, clotted flowers
Outlining desire.

My stubby fingers
Trace fragile networks
Of veins and dreams,
Even now redolent
With plausibility
And surprise.

I imagine you clothed
In brown dungarees, perhaps,
And a cotton shirt to match
The color of your eyes.
Under the carved moons
Of your fingernails
There is soil from the garden
Where you planted beans
And squash.

In the mountains where I live
We plant rice and never wonder
If our lips are too wide.
Our noses too broad or flat.
We could almost be
Brothers, you and I,
Waking at this very hour
Across the waters
After a dream of wild boars
Breaking into the heart
of the labyrinthine forest.

INSOMNIA
FOR JKC

No more
Than an arm's length
Away,
Your body,
Under the two blankets
Whose edges you so
Precisely folded together
Before sleep came,
Wakes in another country.

If I should touch you
Now,
You would think only
That it was your sleeve
Caught in the underbrush
Or the fingers of fern
Drawing you
Deeper into the landscape
Of dreams.

Sitting here
I study
Your sleeping form:
The ripples on the sheets
Are waters I must cross
To follow
Where you have gone.

Your breathing
Becomes wind,
And the vein
Faintly throbbing
On your temple,
Uncertain beacon.
Strange
How it is I, wide-eyed,
That surfaces from an ocean
Of dreams where
Alternately I find
And lose you again,
A thousand times,
An eternity,
Before I beach
My own
Spent body
On the shores
Of morning.

LEAVE-TAKING

Child
Your name dies
Upon my lips
As though the very air
Had taken its
Substance.
Henceforth
No one
Shall say it
Except in pained
Whispers,
Or when a census is taken
And we who live
Must account
For this moment
When you
Are severed from me
Forever.

CURSE

At a funeral,
Aunt sidles up with tea
And the bones of an old story.
She twirls her many rings
Around fingers grown knobby
From years of weaving
And divination
Above the shallow depths
Of her stone mortar.

Her house is full of wooden gods
And crockery, all older than we are.
Her eyes, not yet accustomed
To grief, attempt to resurrect in mine
The terror of an old curse; how sons
Shall father only daughters
Who will marry into oblivion,
How finally our names shall disappear
Upon the wind.

In the next room her only son lies
Wrapped in blankets for the dead.
Flies hover around the garden trees
Burdened with fruit and blood offerings,
Their buzzing audible above
The drone of chanting voices.
In this flood of voices,
I turn and catch a sunlit glimpse

Of my three daughters by the window,
Strong and firm of limb
And clear of face,
Guiltless, who
Will father forth
Whole histories
Of their creation.

ENCOUNTER

Sister Angéle, formidable.
Frowns at the task before her.
Furtively I glance at my
Clipped fingernails, inspect
My shoes for mud.
This is the first day.
Sweat drips dark plumes
Down the backs of blanched blouses,
Clumping at napes.

On the shelves are things called books
Which we are too timid to handle.
On the wall is a map
Where she points out,
Boat-months away, Belgium.
There she picked cowslips on the riverbank
In a time separate
From the grey habit
And heavy brogans.

Shyly, we bring her flowers
From the trails leading
To our homes.
They are wild blooms,
Their petals ringed
With colors of fire.
For the first time,
She smiles.

She enters my dreams,
A book fragrant with words
And pictures in her hand,
Her right arm grown large,
Pushing the slow clouds aside
To write across the chalky blue.
I think about oceans.
I understand desire.

IN GUISAD VALLEY
*FOR EUGENE PUCAY, 90
AND ALICE PUCAY, 84*

We steeled ourselves
For this, years
Before it happened,
Imagining the thinning
Of our breath, the wrists
And ankles admitting
The telltale tremor
On cold mornings
And nights.

No one could have told us
How it would be, how
Our days grow now
Into each other
With surprising ease.

In the mornings,
There is rice
And fish, perhaps
An egg for you;
The papers,
Which I can read
Even now without glasses.
It may take a while
For words to form,
But I remember the names
Of all our friends.

In the front yard
You walk past
The coffee trees
Filming over with
White flowers.
Soon the beans will ripen,
Just as in the days
When you were a schoolgirl
Walking from Bua
To this valley.

Afternoons, we sit
Side by side
In two armchairs
Among the pots of bonsai,
Accomplices even in silence
As we drift down
The lengthening current
Of our thoughts.

Evenings, we retire
And say a prayer
Of simple thanks.
Sometimes I think
It would be nice
To wake one morning
And find ourselves,
Two trees,
Linking limbs
And leafy foliage.

LEGEND

There are many tales
Surrounding this place.

If you stand very still,
If you hollow out a space
In the middle of your thoughts

The way a child waits, shyly,
Almost deferentially,
For the grownups in the crowded parlor
To notice she is there,

You may see one of them
Assemble in the light.

By then, the light itself
Will be changed and muted,
As in a print of sepia.
The voices around you
Will fall differently,
As though
Through layers of moss.

The noon traffic shall melt away
And the stone curb yield
Its asphalt heart
To suddenly reveal
A river:
I can tell you its name
Is *Chanum*.

There will be trees
Newly emerging from mist,
Slender and dark as calligraphies
On new paper.

From the huts
On the other side of the water,
Tongues of smoke shall curl
Skyward, bearing stories
From the hearth
To another world.

There is nothing
To be uncertain of.

It will be possible to move
Beyond the scrim of leaves,
Possible to go so close
To realize the flash of metal
From the hunter's spear
Is not a trick of sunlight,

Before the shaft flies
And the wounded deer falls
With you, inevitably,
Into everyday
Shadow.

CARTOGRAPHER

On this
Brittle ground
I trace a parchment time
And place: here
Among the lines
Are many lives;
The space I briefly
Touch with my index finger
In the heart of a valley,
The dark smudge on the left,
The flap of owl's wing.
Hidden in
The inky shadow
Of mountains I see
Heads lift
From around a fire
To listen
To the low note
Of the herdsman's horn.
If you listen
You shall hear
The dark thunder of hooves,
If you lean
Into the wind, scent
The nearness of
The watering-hole,
As a thumbnail sliver
Of moon
Slides into place
In the sky.

CONFIGURING THE GODS
AND OTHER POEMS

A SENSE OF BALANCE

> *Our middle*
> *is our extreme.*
> —Hartman

Gravity, they say: the apple falling
With a thud upon the bare,
Unwitting head, to illustrate a certain given—
Precarious anchorage of flesh to bone,
Of bone to rock and dappled sun,
Such rootedness itself
Not merely being human
Or other nature. For instance, see
How the white shapes of buildings
And their spires and domes
Apparently connive to arc one
Imperceptible, sweeping line against the blue.
Fields and towns, the swirling surf
Rushing continually away from you,
Feet pacing semblance of solid turf:
All cultivate unerring sense
Of balance here. For all earth's gravity
Is nothing but a wish
To moor and to attach, to grow
The simple root, like grass,
Everything else is grafted so—but us.
For we equate the state
Of weightlessness with grace, are caught
Up in designs of flying mystics
And of whirling dervishes
But still, must notify the soil

Of our own kinship—
Primal—with its weighted core
While grimly walking on a razor's edge
Where earth and air unnerve, divide:
How could we know the pendulum
Would swing this wide?

REMEMBERING A DEATH
FOR M

And you were almost legend
(Not one we meant to fashion,
Though fate perhaps has had its way)
Whom we referred to with the proper awe
That let us know
How in the end, it was persistence
We would have: the final thing,
Lush fruit in hand, sun
Beating down as always,
Emblazoning hills, framing
One patch of sky with salutary boughs.

Something has departed though,
And we are ill-prepared
For how the high wind, fern and mold
Insinuate how even mountains change
Their habit. Once your refuge,
Now merciless in heat or cold
They stand, testament
To all the ground behind us
Tilled and piled high
With the bones of tears
Pressed between thoughtful fingers
And our archaic, stumbling prose.

Now and then a tremor
From an anger throbbing in some city street,
From the unexpected bomb or rain of fire,
Will cleave the stony silence of your hills.
Above them the pines stand unruffled, still;
From them we have learned to say
Now there are no cowards,
Traitors, heroes—
There are only men.

SEPTEMBER

Always, I am stupefied
By air: when burrowed
In a room, throwing
Coverlets of leaf and shade about me,
To press, press
The sound of rain forever out of hearing
Till arms have tired
And memory forgotten
What it held—
        Cup of joy,
        Plane of wood,
        Stone, water,
        Sun, cold—

How a shutter will always
Open somewhere,
Remorselessly
Spilling some scent to enthrall me:
A cistern in the yard,
Bunches of fruit in trees
Breaking irresistibly out of their flesh
Into the sudden and dangerous warmth.
And I stumble to fling
The casements open wholly
To see September sunshine
On rain-soaked streets,
Feel fingers of sun poke through my limbs,
Till I stand
Timorous and still

As a bird
Under the high,
Windswept dome
Of heaven.

CONFIGURING THE GODS

Our fingers inscribe a ritual
Upon all they touch, seeking passage to
An unmapped chamber in the mind
But dimly remembered now—
A room where rapture lay upon the flagstones
Like sunlight on the glass,
Denser than dustmotes
Or the air without, bending the grass.

A song pressed hesitantly on the ivory,
Child's cheek cupped in nightly ceremony
Or smoothed to sleep;
Hands touching hands, describing
The outward form of trees and lives:
And yet we fail to ferment, leaven, swim
Above the cumbrous counterpoise of flesh
And self, nor catch one last, remembered, golden
Glimpse of gods disappearing
Beyond the hill's dark rim.

THE ALCHEMIST'S STONE

From what inviolate depths or pools
Shall we attempt to draw you, how
Read the runes that with the emerald waters flow?
Stars burn—but coldly, deciphering hulls
Of vessels by the rocky shore.

Assemble here the dust and shingle;
Spore and seed, fillet and tendril
Of scraggly weed. What medieval fire
Or potent creed shall mingle
These, to render the solar ray:

Essence of sun, not gold,
A way to finally mold blind night
And yield the rising forms
Of trees, ferns, clouds? Enthralled
By rumors of a chemistry

To transubstantiate one
Transparency of flesh to seamless soul,
We keep watch in the clearings, stoke
Tinder of deciduous bark and bone,
Pondering how fire's a way to be reborn.

VIGIL

> *What is a man in the Infinite?*
> *. . . a mean between nothing and everything.*
> —Pascal, *Pensees*

No matter that the eye
Has shifted space, receding
Into a seething cataract from which,
Now, it peers: memory,
More real sometimes than sun,
And something un-
Definable (itself an eye)
Batter themselves against
The human carapace.
What then? The inward I
Surveys the landscape it must cross:
Dyslexic sea, hydra of self
Wrapped in a faery haze—
And apprehension becomes like this:
How the ant shoulders a clod
And the wolverine its prey,
And you follow
To what hollow,
Seeking the spoor
Through the labyrinthine trail
Of fern and grass.

Waking is finding
Shadows of leaves splayed cool
Upon the helpless brow
And feeling, not sensing where
Sunbeams are moving

Behind the curtained grille.
Soon the moment's peace
Will be as difficult to comprehend
As the heat that now is not.

ROSES FROM THE SEA

Would Gabriel Garcia
Have recognized their scent?
Up from the sea and floating
Into this vast, consuming dark,
As lights in windows flicker on.

In the city half-sprawled, half-imagined
As some great chiaroscuroed garden under glass,
Fingers stumble from under bedclothes,
Spring up from laps, drop
The encircled glass—
Uncertain still to thrill
To strange new currents breaking
Through long-deadened air.

Their images emerge and then withdraw
Upon unceasing waves:
Icons of flowers and palms rustling,
Parting the damask air.
And in our sleep we dream
Of things reverting to what once
They were: cipher of sea and land,
Where, turning, we sense
A garden there
Whose foliage glistens
With the sun's old,
Fleeting gold.

ADAGIO

How often has it been told, the common failure
Of the architects of dreams: something it was we sought
More than the blueprint, or the fine
Endurance of the work of steel. Fraught
With the fever of what it would be like,
Stone and the Word grown
Opalescent and bright,
Hands learning to shape whole
Syllables of speech, meeting of eyes—
How is it then no passion seals all acts, how sight
Never means vision? The treasure sought
Is laid away in a time-encrusted box.
Forgetfulness, and then
The searching for what once lay there
Like flash of new silver, or the clasp to fasten
Thought at last to the deed itself.
And it is true
We leave our faith in hidden things like these,
Moving perpetually out of shadows and into
The preludes to a frail kind of peace.

CLARITY

> *O rider mounted astride time,*
> *What is your body but time itself?*

One knows by the involuntary gleam
Of surfaces within a darkened room
How one must move
Just so: but only by instinct,
And instinct needs a world
To tutor it. Like the way, perhaps,
A sunbeam dazzles
And defines the dust, or how
The sky outlines all images
Which use it as a screen.

But there are other screens:
A greying checkerboard of days
And corridors that wander.
To keep the vision stark, they say
I should return to things
Their proper names: solidify,
Amass the splintered parts,
Reconstitute the elemental essences
From what they're not;
So that a leaf is no mere leaf
Nor subterfuge of mind,
But more than thought, startling with its green
And feeling one's way's no longer
Dodging the solid thing
But knowing that we make our way
Although without, worlds spin.

A WEAVING SONG

>   *Tabi ni yande*
>   *yume wa kareno wo*
>   *kakemeguro*

>   (On a journey, ill—
>   O'er fields all withered
>   Dreams go wandering still.)
>   —Matsuo Basho

In search of seasons
That will prove indelible as time,
I have trained my hunger
To a weaving-wheel.
Nightly my hand plies the secret loom,
But I am traveller still
Though it is others who depart
Or who withdraw, uncertain
Of how fingers
Can bend to fashion love
From all they touch—or anguish.

Some need compels I memorize
The smell of surf borne from an alien shore
By errant winds into these stony hills;
The sound of water dripping
Into some hidden pool,
The blight of stars beneath a garden frond.

In deep of night I wake to sense
A chord vibrating in the air, the way
Buds are resting in their pewter vase:

At noon my eyes behold
The wonder of doves
Fluttering in the frieze
Of noon heat
And the breathless trees.

But even these move: birds scatter
And shadows shift their purple weight
From leaves and boughs,
And no seam shows.
Daily my feet repeat the old
Familiar paths, and lead me back
To my own hearth.
There the heart notes and executes
The shuttle's silent exercise
Upon taut and comprehending threads.

Outside, in the hills, love roams.

WOMAN FROM THE NORTH

See: these are tokens of mountains
I bear on my arms;
Trees I love,
The lightning flash,
Terraces lightly sleeping
In power—
Proud heirlooms I wear
Upon my breasts.

There arms dance, too:
Whirl
Patterns of prayer
To a mountain god,
Lift
A sky's worth
Of cabbages,
    newspapers,
      cans of water,
Swing
    a baby hammock
      under canopy of breasts—

Age-old font
Of strength,
Enduring
As the mountains
That mark my flesh
Down to the sole

That burnishes the soil,
The gnarled
And beautiful
Feet.

DISCLOSURES

MOUNT SANTO TOMAS

These are the foothills
That the deer scaled,
Shedding gold as it ran.
On the other side,
The sea heard its braying
And turned to listen,
And the dogs leapt
But did not know what possessed them.
The signs were read:
The faces of stones on the path,
The cusped moon floating
In the sky. All breathed *"Kabunian."*
The omen birds rose
From the reeds,
Circling the dark peak.
The ground was cleared,
Saleng heaped on the leaping fire
By many hands.
Gongs strung pulses
Through the hushed air,
Women stirred up wind
With chanting voices.
Prayers were danced
Into the soft earth, pressed
Into syllables by arms and wrists:
Later that day, rain fell.

IMPROVISATION

*Your house burned down
sometime ago . . .*

A change of season, rain, water
The color of mud—and all the markers
Of a life have blurred
To indistinction.
By a stove blazing pine and cypress boughs
My fingers will sift with as much patience
As they can muster, through pieces
Of a snapped geography.
Nights before sleep takes me
I shall try on hands and knees
To recognize what former landscapes
Have been buffed to the color of wheat,
The shape of broken hills.
Here is the rider, and here
The carriage with its bells
And gaudy ornaments. Nearby
A horse the color of dried reeds
Whinnies and disappears
Into the sedge.
It was only a matter of time,
This remembering of how
Every surface breaks and creeps
Under its load of items given,
Items received, children born
And grieved: now
Everything unravelled
Must be rebuilt.

MONSOON

Nefastus, the moment
At which all curves coincide
In descendence: the lane disappearing
From view, wind ducking and flapping
Under the eaves, sun drowning
In a sheath of rain.
Mornings are clothed in auspicious beginnings,
Always persuading with ease
And with light that the day
Shall be like no other:
By noon they have turned
Into various rehearsals of death.
Over the land the colors are ashen,
On our ledge the mantle of blight.
Like planets struggling
With the weight of their orbits,
We drag ourselves through the rooms
Touching old books, shaking out poems
Touching their hiding-places to cut
Through the thickening air.
If we were not who we are
It would be simple to wait for a moon
And under its light bury the heart
Of a chicken, read the bitter tracery
In its sac of bile; draw a thread
Through a black sow's liver
And count the years remaining to us,
Or the number of children to come—
Sometimes, we manage.

Other times, something
Must give—like the safety
Of not looking death
In the eye.

FROM EVE

*To have been one
of many ribs
and to be chosen.
To grow into something
quite different . . .*
—Linda Pastan

Radiance tempts
From every tree.
The lure of color is too much
To bear, the rustle of leaves
Would mesmerize a stone.
What defense could my hands fashion?
Already the athame drips
With blood, my daughters' names
Blaze in my ears: Ishtar,
Diana, Demeter, Circe—
Everyone shall burn somehow
For this. Even I
Have been assigned a place
In the gnarled fretwork of dreams
Yet I will tell you
That I own no book of shadows,
No bags of bitter charm
Or mandrake root. The serpent
Sheds its scales,
Working out the problems
Of its own transcendence.
I want only the promise of stars
Buried deep in the apple's belly.

MATEO

This was no prophecy;
It only came to pass
The way myths flower
In velvet, mossy silence.
Picture this, then:
Thin drizzle from sky
Pewter as a *sillasi*.
Sputtering flame,
Dishes of boar meat,
Old men, spreading
The weave of looser years
Across drawn knees.

This was the time
For conjuring tales;
Smoke curled
Into pine-shapes,
Stone-shapes,
The glint of hunting-knives.

The young hunter
Leant apart.
Outside the hut,
The gods were listening
Through the cracks.
A deer brayed.
Sun broke gold
Through clouds.

POEM FOR GRANDMOTHERS, MOTHERS AND DAUGHTERS

> *Here's yesterday, last year—*
> *Palm-spear and lily distinct as flora in the vast*
> *Windless threadwork of tapestry.*
> —Sylvia Plath

Your figures stamp across the paths of memory:
The flailing of your hands, repeating the motion
That trees make when sudden winds slam
Their open palms onto the blistered bark
To shake the sweetness out of summer.

Gathering the fallen fruits
And setting them aside,
We bend our heads against the tearing air;
The blood beats in our ears. We take
Our places round the table, raise
Glasses in a silent toast
To necessary bonds we share. See how
Each tendril on our heads
Soaks deeply up the generations' store—
Decanted wine of umbrage and of gall,
The anise flower blooming into taste:
The root and passion of us all.

HARVEST-EVE

Silence is speech cupped round
The syllables we have forgotten.
The cold pins us taut under covers
And vainly we think
Of what kindling to blaze,
To erase it.

A new moon rises,
Leaking its wet shine
Through tin sheeting
And onto the woven blankets.
Your voice shakes free of the silence,
But only for a moment.

"Tomorrow,
We dig up the potatoes."
The sound is loose earth
Falling back upon the ground.

My fingers burrow now
And find your hand.
Drifting off to sleep, I curl
My fingers firmly around yours
As I would lift a tuber
From the field,
And weigh it
Against the emptiness of stone.

PICTURE-TAKING IN BESAO

The toothless elder crouches
In the doorway's shadowed skirts.
He is afraid the strange, black
Metal amulet hanging heavy
From the stranger's neck
Will pleat his soul and paper his breath.
The children say it does not hurt;
They laugh to see how he persists
In holding converse with the ether
Of ideas from a trackless land.
"You live in the hollows
Of your cheeks. Come dance!" they mock.
But no—it is enough for him
To sit within the doorway's shadowed frame
And feel the grim and brittle outlines
Of his soul press strange
Reassurance round his bones.
A wild bird, plumage red,
Connives to catch his rheumy eye
As it commits its body
To the wrinkled sky.

FROM AN ALBUM

> *Now there is no news from that world*
> *Nobody misses us or asks for us*
> *It is so dark there, that at night*
> *Window or no window, it is all the same,*
> *In the flowing water there is no trace*
> *of our reflection.*
> —CS Taranci

All that I have known
Of childhood has bowed out
And left this room.
The last piece of furniture
Has been boxed and carted away,
And only the wood gleams darkly,
The hard, bright floor inviting
A lowering of head or cheek
To the heart of its emptiness.
Without looking I know
That an ageing moon is in the sky,
Riding towards the sun
That will not be reached
Until morning. By then
It will be too late,
All out of reach, tucked
Into hiding,
Moulting,
Transforming
Into the various nostalgias
Of forthcoming seasons.
A short walk, the opening
Of a door shall marry my fate

To that of the eucalyptus
And the crackling brake.
Branches shoot their last wild runners out
To pluck dreams split onto the dark.
The landscape circles close,
Already it circles towards noon
When the world stands as if without shadow,
Composing itself
For the coming of sorrow.

OMAIRA

> *Sometime in mid-morning,*
> *the girl suddenly shuddered,*
> *raised her shoulders and died*
> *of heart failure.*
> —Rescuer on 13-year-old Omaira
> Sanchez's death after 60 hours
> in the mud, in Colombia

The heat is not because of sun
But bodies hovering around me,
Armed with paper and various wires
That they would have me speak into.
I have nothing to say—only
That we lived on *Calle Luz*,
And there were lemon trees
In my backyard.
Are these men disappointed?

My head whirls
Through the long day,
Quieting only at night
When everyone is gone
And the moon, grey
Splintered moon,
Floats on the glossy water.

My hands are white
Above the mud. They
Are so still, I wonder
If they are really mine
Or the ghosts of summer's

Magnolias, shrivelled
In the wind?

The screams are almost gone.
I wait for my brief life
To stretch before me,
Like a glimpse of shore
Before the plunge.
Nothing happens, though;
Only my eye, fixed on
The teetering cornice
Of *La Playa,* preparing to catch
Another tremor.
Forgive me,
It is my first time
To die.

BURYING KINJA

A cloud-flecked sky holds back
Its attitude of rain, watching
As once, twice, the heavy blankets
Are folded around the body.
The relatives gather slowly,
Testing their hearts against silence:
Women with dark kerchiefs,
Men in grey coats.

The ochre beads are laid
On Kinja's hollow breast—
So many sons, daughters,
Brothers, hurtled back
From distant years.

The cracked stones hoard
Their secret, milky light,
Saying only "Matriarch,
Mother, Touchstone,"
Words that will never show
The girlhood braiding finally
Into opacity of lives.

So many offerings:
Raw meat suspended from the trees,
And in the courtyard a sow
Shuddering surrender
Beneath the wooden spike.

Sudden sun blanches the red plain.
Each cheek is daubed
With ceremonial blood.
The smells of death
Have jewelled the rank air.

THIRTY-THIRD YEAR

> *Each step we take is more than a journey*
> *We have no need to be in a hurry . . .*
> —P. Reverdy

The journey is your favorite
Metaphor. In each place you look,
An emblem drops like fruit
From some unseen tree,
And you stretch out your
Begging bowl.
Your heart wishes such fullness.
The green smudge of trees
Ringing a pale sky
Will shed its charities soon.
When even that has gone,
The village lane flanked
By sleepy houses
On whose porches dogs
Flick lazy tails and women spread
Their wash to dry,
For you will burn a secret blaze.
What landscapes do not know
This restlessness?
It is merely the wind perhaps,
Or the tongues of the sea
Hissing into this valley,
Saying, "What you seek is not here,
Press on."

AT MARYHEIGHTS

>   . . . *Climb or let go! Thou hast had Time enough,
> and the patience of Thy Father is exhausted.*
> —David Foster, Moonlite

The flowers rise in columns here,
Trained to arch their bodies to the light
Among the cages of the pigeons
And doves, and the lone eagle
Agonizing in his fenced-in-tree.
You say: Clearly this
Is no place to speak of present
Or of future; everything is past,
Everything has happened, the priests
That pace these petalled paths
Inscribe an old medieval order
On these stones. Even now,
Each tree we pass has claimed our gestures,
Clothing them in bark, the rings
To count whole histories on.
A twig falls, breaks underfoot,
A bird flies, whose trajectory and fall
Were calculated in the dark
Before we even rose to morning.

And in reply I tell you
How my lungs are drinking in this air,
And look—how the grass refuses to die
Beneath the surest of our tramplings.
The wind's a long skein where night
And day are spiriting the woods'

And our secrets away,
And we will never know them, never
Ever guess if breaking off
A lily from its blue-green stalk
Shall spell our certain doom
Or restoration.
Rows of flowering bean
Divide our steps, the thin screen
Of our metaphysic bearing up
Under the voyaging sun;
And still we are together
On a landscape
Incandescent, human.

AFTER MOVIES

The stairs would lead
Into another kind of dark
Where dreams would happen:
The fawn losing its mother
In the snow, mirrors
Tricking a room into uncertain life,
The witch's crooked fingers
Polishing an apple
To a wicked glow.
The heat must penetrate
The ring of thorn and fire,
And in its falling swoon
Win back the healing herb,
The song of nightingales.
Bearing such boons,
We cleave the dark
That marks the end,
The curtain falling.
Through evening's muted streets
Our souls hurry ahead
But towards what, we have
No real strength to know:
Lights pour from every open window
Like grace, or like the scenes
Of something burning.

COMING OF AGE

*A hungry man craves a handful of barley
but sated he deems the whole earth straw.*

At times I think my life
Is something that my hands
Are finally growing accustomed to:
The daily surenesses that walls
Offer, the whorls on wood that threaten
To run and fuse at any moment
Yet keep their place, air

That one no longer needs to stir or pulse
For rumors (believing that these
Will announce their coming with pennants
Bright as a bled horizon)
Of a heartbeat or a footfall issuing
From far ahead up a path, disclosures
That shall tell the way, whether

Into the heart of the flower drooping
In its shot blue vase upon the mantel
Or of the mountains
Whose silences are peril and promise.

Beyond the shutters the last sunflowers
Bury themselves in dripping foliage;
Blind fingers span the length
Of darkening sky, imagining its corners
Succumb to the wetness of the weather,
Offering memory and desire

Like fatted pigs to the lightning,
Waiting, waiting
For its cobalt crack.

SIGHTINGS

SIGHTINGS

In our language,
There is no word
For autumn.
Leaves fall
Seemingly at random
Through summer
And the long wet
Season, this way
Rendering one day
Indecipherable
From another.

In the middle of the year,
This unexpected heat
Has the power to delude
The senses.
The far script of hills
Is suddenly tangible,
The night no longer
Muffles
The scent of flowers
With rain.

For one brief,
Improbable moment
I imagine
The years
Falling away from my life

Like so many leaves
Into darkness.

And, as I give
Myself over to sleep
Like an after-image
Under closed lids
A pure, dark outline
Flickers and
Is gone.

PARCHMENT

> *"the true is the conjunction*
> *between being and seeming."*

Everywhere, it is summer.
In the distance the fire trees
Smolder into bloom.
Leaves crackle. What mysteries
Shrivel on their tongues
Depart like smoke
Through air.
The sky is one
Blue cipher, a blank
Filled in with such frank color
That inwardly I flinch
And shade my eyes.
Below it there are hills
Of terracotta, porous
As the skin of arms or thighs,
A language some would trust
More than the words
Assembling on this landscape.
And yet, they are no different
From the season's heat
Or sensuous spoils:
On paper parched as any soil
They spill their thousand odors, rush
To their fulfillment and desire
As even now this poem flames
And dies, leaving no ashes,
Only the bone of memory
Scorched clean again.

OPENWORK

The woman bends
At her embroidery, counting
The number of stitches
Before her lover's signal.
Already she has heard
His horse's hooves crash
Through the underbrush of pages,
Unmindful of the scent
Of *caimitos* flowering
Upon the tree outside her window.
For the first time she notices
How the carved heraldic flowers
Twine their hearts around the table
With its one lighted taper.
Soon, very soon,
This moment will fuse
With others from another time,
And faces vaguely resembling hers
Will crowd the page to listen
To the tale of how
The moon was bright
For fleeing lovers
And how the only clue
Was a muslin shawl
Edged with fine
Openwork.

THE SEND-OFF

Suddenly it is time.
The men roll out the flowers,
Taking the hothouse air
And clearing the room of all
Except keenest contrition.

In the confusion
So like that which precedes
Boat rides and airplane flights,
There is baggage to account for,
Last-minute messages, the panic
Of possible amnesia.

By grief the sky
Has been reduced to a square
Of streaky blue.
There could be rain,
But even that would be
Good for omens.

So we file past, arranging
Your hat, an extra pair of shoes,
A wallet which someone has remembered
To stuff with bills and loose change.
There are sheets, matches, a candle.
Our throats fill with salt,
Our fingers with unmoored vowels.

The hearse opens
To receive you, dark
As a womb or a tunnel
Whose end, though we stand
On tiptoe, remains veiled
In deepest shadow.

SAGADA

For Joey

Loneliness is not like Sagada.
The road, like one perpetual promise,
Is strewn with rocks and flowers
And the tender needles of young pine.

My thoughts flit swiftly
Through the crosshatches of sunlight.
Outside the window, the eucalyptus breathes.
I see again the yellow dip of clouds
Pointing toward Besao.
Gongs ring out their wedding joy,
And the sound fans the rice in the paddies.

Between loved ones a thousand fibers
Pronounce one harmony.

CHILD ASLEEP

For Jenny

In the streets below,
Two drunks, shadows plastered on the pavement
By the yellow ooze of light;
Ribald laughter and the clatter of a can
Ripping the mauve stillness.

Sighing, you turn,
A mittened hand extended
To touch the rippled surface of a dream.

LAKE DANOM

Night, dimming the flame beyond the hill,
Genuflects beneath the ancient trees.
Gazing long at rooftops
Through a swirl of fog and a fragmented eye,
I quilt the pieces of a ragged globe.
What then was it,
That breathed its name to me?
The sudden leap, inexplicable bursting,
Blooming, and the voice I knew,
Singing like a keen wind in my veins?
Night dims, my vision fails.
(I sense the treachery of friends,
Faith prostituted by the heart.)

And so I come to listen
To the lake water, its cool song,
Remembering what time is,
Feeling space recede and sky broaden
Into singularity.
Surely, the wandering will come to an end.
O my heart, gather up your weeds
And celebrate your harvest with hope.

UNTITLED

Morning comes—a tumble of magnolias
Over the sleeping hills.
The scent is everywhere, everywhere,
A strange compelling magic, that now
Causes the eye to reflect a light
Purer than its own;
And it is prayer enough
To contemplate birds winging sunward
And the white blooms sustaining in the heat.

ON THE BOULEVARD

It seems time for the pale shades to filter in,
For the water to break once over the low stones
Before evening.
On the white cushions I have lain
In my silk kimono, reading Rimbaud,
Waiting for the clink of ice cubes in your glass.
If you must know, I am watching the lights
Come out over the city.
I think of yesterday,
And the boy's hand thrust in the car window;
With five small, weary fingers,
Rebuking the long coolness of my day.
It was early morning on the boulevard
And over the ramparts the sea
Broke mournfully.

WISH

Not whether one is free—
That is the door that opens
Only to revolve upon itself.
Rather, to go
Into the wild seas, down
Into the valleys,
To scour the lunar landscape
With a shard of bone
And then,
Between eaves of silence
Coax forth
A brave
Calligraphy of songs.

PASSAGES

Ruptured sky and ruptured earth,
And I am dumb though flame devour my head;
Within this cell the multifoliate tongues
Press close, invoking memory
To lead me to the flower in the fire.
O how astonishing to speak in tongues;
It is as though I catch a glance, deep in,
Of mirrors in the mind, concealing nuances
I had not thought were there.
Row after row of images appoint themselves
Upon the glass: the frozen pause, the open stare,
Pictures from a child's uncertain past
That mingle here with compromises made
In mid-November. I remember the dust,
Heavy as time, settling in corners; spectres, shadows,
And the certainty that I must not stay.
For here too a way of life
Begins, touching many sheeted faces,
And the frayed edges
Of a sleep that can no longer last.

LAST SUPPER

For Papa

An early supper of fish and rice:
You pass the coffee cups
Steaming with a blessed warmth,
And we sit in armchairs
In the living room.

Pattering down the upturned fringe
Of light upon the stair,
My children come to hug goodnight,
Smelling of bread, milk,
And the fragrance of cotton sheets.

You smile and pat the tender heads
With hands grave and subtly shadowed
As the limestone cliffs.
That day in April when we
Climbed their ash-white sides
To fly kites,
You scooped great armfuls
Of the laundered air—
And, feeling lavish,
Pointed out the creamy
Billow of an angel-cloud;
Father and daughter succumbing
To the sorcery of laughter
And of air.

Here, where we sit,
Moonlight mingles with lamplight
Like some benediction
Out of a cloudless sky.
Again, we are alone.
I watch you with protective, longing eye,
My heart entangled forever
In linen sheets.

Suddenly your thoughts
Are clear to me.
I, too, hear the beating of wings.
As you ascend the stair the light
Pours silver on your hair.
I drink the bitter liquid in my cup, Father,
And feel

The trees that in the garden bend,
The dripping of the fountain-drops,
The thorns that breathe communion with the rose—
Are all within the chalice of my world
Bleeding with the weight of love.

TRYST

It was dawn, blue and chill
And silver, and the scent
Of trumpet-flowers marshalling the remnants
Of a harvest moon
Across the eastern sky.
Behind the pillars, on a bench,
Waiting for the bus
I watch a blur of wings—
Birds reeling in the naked air,
The sudden shock of morning.

Out of a world of shapes and shadows
And centers that move about at will,
We have come presumably as birds
Who moult their plumage of desire and pain.
And my heart contracted, was afraid,
After the long ride over the ravines
And limestone faces pointing out a cobalt sky;
We might not find our Simurgh there.
Through dusty villages
And sad, deserted groves,
We chase the shadow of the peacock's fan
Unfurling over silent mountains, silent seas.

In time, we shall resume
The customary pose of only men.
We shall clasp hands at table,
Embrace in bed,

And press the lonely wind into our aching sides;
We walk the asphalt earth by day,
Dispensing crumbs of laughter, crumbs of love,
Each terrain still as unfamiliar as our selves.

A few quiet days and nights—
For watching shadows fall
In russet planes upon the sheets,
For warmth and touch,
A bit of serious talk
And shelter from the ancient pines—
Might quell the thrashing of our souls
That seek to negotiate
The spangle-point of light.

The bus lurches on;
Ensconced in our window seat
We watch the passing landscape.
Rounding a bend we startle
A flock of birds.
They rise and briefly hover
In the infinite blue.

DANCER AT THE BARRE

The head, inclined,
Rests on an invisible lover's arm;
The hands, seeking wood.
Find only air.
The fulcrum's not there—
Neither in mirror, nor hall,
Nor the patterns of music
Like lace on the wall.
But these, too, are gathered
Like leaves in a field,
Under a lone tree
Whose branches are stirred
By wind and water
Sky and earth.
A gesture of arm, a tensing in air:
A softness succeeds—
The world's axis scooped
In the point of her shoe.

LANDSCAPES

For a Second Anniversary

It will begin quite ordinarily, I know:
A deepening blue at edge of window,
These same brown walls
Containing me and you.

Out at the sky's rim, like a Gauguin,
A languid and tropical cloud.
No wind blows through the sparse grass,
Nothing trembles in the air or earth—
A dawn caught dreaming
Between dreams.

Around us crowd the fabrics and the furniture
Of waking life, named, colored,
Solid and unimpeachable,
Even in sleep laving our bodies where we lie.
The landscapes we inhabit
Are multiplied by two:
One, the cloud again
And bare-armed women, brown by an aquamarine sea.
Then, the world beyond the water
Or the sky, interior and dry:
Where no air is,
How distant can we fly?

The water must move and shimmer,
Draw the noon heat down into its long shadow;
At length the women's hands must cease their idling
And divining amongst grass and flowers
Blazing forth their own small suns,
Realizing that the light of our perceiving
May dissolve the borders of their canvas sky.

Our own skies hold us rapt
But free to move beyond the frames
Into the archipelagoes of commerce,
Pain and love, to hunt
For the petals of ourselves
Still lost or dreaming in the grass.

So then, beloved, the time will pass,
Motion immutable, irrevocable:
Still, there is the water
And the invitation
To alter the posture
Of our earth.